FIRST TOUCH SOCCER

C.A.
RIVER PLATE

BY

MARK STEWART

NORWOOD HOUSE PRESS

Chicago, Illinois

Norwood House Press

P.O. Box 316598 • Chicago, Illinois 60631
For more information about Norwood House Press please visit our website at
www.norwoodhousepress.com or call 866-565-2900.

Photography and Collectibles:
The trading cards and other memorabilia assembled in the background for this book's cover and interior pages are all part of the author's collection and are reproduced for educational and artistic purposes.

All photos courtesy of Associated Press except the following individual photos and artifacts (page numbers): Rothmans Football (6) El Grafico (10 top), D.C. Thomson (10 bottom), The Upper Deck Company LLC (11 top), Figurine Panini (11 middle), Futera Trade Cards Ltd. (11 bottom), Author's Collection (16, 23), ProMatch (22).

Cover image: Agustin Marcarian/Associated Press

Designer: Ron Jaffe
Series Editor: Mike Kennedy
Content Consultants: Michael Jacobsen and Jonathan Wentworth-Ping
Project Management: Black Book Partners, LLC
Editorial Production: Lisa Walsh

LIBRARY OF CONGRESS CATALOGING-IN-PUBLICATION DATA
Names: Stewart, Mark, 1960 July 7- author.
Title: C.A. River Plate / By Mark Stewart.
Description: Chicago Illinois : Norwood House Press, 2017. | Series: First
   Touch Soccer | Includes bibliographical references and index. | Audience:
   Age 5-8. | Audience: K to Grade 3.
Identifiers: LCCN 2016058205 (print) | LCCN 2017005795 (ebook) | ISBN
   9781599538679 (library edition : alk. paper) | ISBN 9781684040865 (eBook)
Subjects: LCSH: River Plate (Athletic club)--History--Juvenile literature.
Classification: LCC GV943.6.R53 S84 2017 (print) | LCC GV943.6.R53 (ebook) |
   DDC 796.334/640982--dc23
LC record available at https://lccn.loc.gov/2016058205

This publication is intended for educational purposes and is not affiliated with any team, league, or association including: Club Atletico River Plate, Argentine Football Association, CONMEBOL, or the Federation Internationale de Football Association (FIFA).

302N--072017
Manufactured in the United States of America in North Mankato, Minnesota.

CONTENTS

Words in **bold type** are defined on page 24.

Leonardo Pisculichi and Carlos Sanchez celebrate a goal during a 2015 match.

MEET C.A. RIVER PLATE

Buenos Aires is the largest city in Argentina and one of the largest in South America. The city is home to Club Atlético River Plate. The "athletic" club is named after Rio de la Plata, the river that flows past Buenos Aires. Members play a number of sports, but the club is best known for its soccer team.

Fans in Argentina sometimes call the team "The Millionaires." Many years ago, River Plate was the richest team in the region. Today, the club is still very rich—in talent and history.

TIME MACHINE

The River Plate club started in 1901. During the 1930s, the team hired some of South America's top players. River Plate also built a great **youth program**.

Within a few years, River Plate became so good at scoring goals that fans began calling the club La Maquina, which is Spanish for The Machine. River Plate's best players include Bernabe Ferreyra, Amadeo Carrizo, **Daniel Passarella**, and Javier Saviola.

DANIEL PASSARELLA
ARGENTINA

Yeah! Javier Saviola fires up his teammates during a 2001 match.

Thousands of fans live close enough to El Monumental to walk to River Plate matches.

BEST SEAT IN THE HOUSE

River Plate has played its home matches on the same field since 1938. The stadium is named after Antonio Vespucio Liberti, the man who ran the club for many years. Many fans call it El Monumental, which is Spanish for the "huge" or "awesome" place. The stadium holds more than 75,000 fans. The **national team** of Argentina also plays its home matches there.

COLLECTOR'S CORNER

These collectibles show some of the best River Plate players ever.

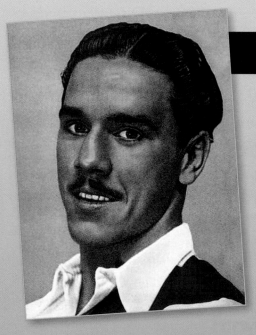

JOSE MANUEL MORENO

Forward
1935–1944 & 1946–1948
Moreno was one of the best players in the world. He was the star of the great La Maquina teams.

ANGEL LABRUNA

Forward
1939–1959
Labruna scored 317 goals for River Plate. He later coached the club to a league title.

ANGEL LABRUNA

ENZO FRANCESCOLI

Midfielder
1983–1986 & 1994–1997
Francescoli scored many amazing goals for River Plate. He was named the top player in South America twice.

UBALDO FILLOL

Goalkeeper
1974–1983
Fillol was one of the finest keepers in South America. In 1978, he helped Argentina win the World Cup.

HERNAN CRESPO

Forward
1993–1996
Crespo was a great attacking player. He led River Plate to the 1996 South American title.

WORTHY OPPONENTS

About three out of every four soccer fans in Argentina root for River Plate or Boca Juniors. Boca Juniors also plays its matches in Buenos Aires, about 30 minutes away. When the two teams meet, everything in the city seems to stop. Fans call their matches Superclasicos. In South America, nothing comes close to the excitement of a Superclasico.

Sebastian Driussi beats a Boca Juniors player to the ball during a 2016 match.

Club Ways

If you buy a ticket for a match at El Monumental, don't get too comfortable in your seat. River Plate fans stand from the beginning of the game to the end. They cheer for their players and scream at the referees. They bring bright flags and homemade banners. When they go home it takes a gigantic clean-up crew to get it ready for the next game.

The game hasn't begun yet, but River Plate fans have already begun to make a mess!

These River Plate players went on to star for top clubs all over the world:

1 **Enzo Francescoli** • Racing Club • Paris, France

2 **Marcelo Gallardo** • A.S. Monaco F.C. • Principality of Monaco

3 **Omar Sivori** • Juventus F.C. • Turin, Italy

4 **Alfredo Di Stefano** • →
Real Madrid C.F. • Madrid, Spain

5 **Radamel Falcao** • F.C. Porto • Porto, Portugal

6 **Ariel Ortega** • Fenerbahce S.K. • Istanbul, Turkey

7 **Oscar Mas** • America de Cali • Cali, Colombia

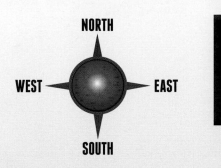

NORTH

WEST   EAST

SOUTH

MAP OF EUROPE

1

5   4

2   3

River Plate's home stadium is in Buenos Aires, Argentina.

6

7

WORLD MAP

The River Plate crest is easy to spot on Leonardo Pisculichi's home uniform.

KIT AND CREST

River Plate's uniform has hardly changed since the 1930s. Players wear a white shirt with a single red stripe and black shorts. The club's away **kit** changes from year to year. It is usually red and black. The club's crest shows a shield with a red stripe and the letters CARP. They stand for Club Atlético River Plate.

WE WON!

The Copa Libertadores tournament is played each year to decide the best club in South America. River Plate won for the first time in 1986. The club won the championship again in 1996. River Plate won its third Copa Libertadores in 2015. The final match was played in a rainstorm. Lucas Alario scored the winning goal on an amazing header. River Plate went on to win by a score of 3–0.

Marcelo Barovero and Fernando Cavenaghi kiss the Copa Libertadores after winning the tournament in 2015. River Plate also won in 1986 and 1996.

FOR THE RECORD

These River Plate players have won the top award in South America:

South American Footballer of the Year

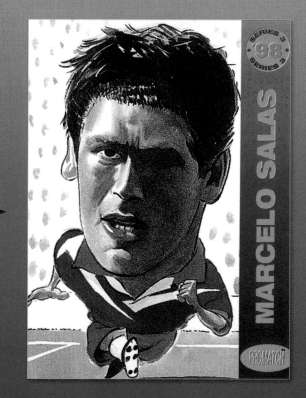

1984   Enzo Francescoli

1986   Antonio Alzamendi

1995   Enzo Francescoli

1997   **Marcelo Salas** ●————————————➤

1999   Javier Saviola

2014   Teofilo Gutierrez

2015   Carlos Sanchez

River Plate has won more than 40 championships!

Primera Division*

36 championships (from 1920 to 2014)

Copa Libertadores**

1986
1996
2015

Copa Sudamericana**

2014

Intercontinental Cup

1986

Adolfo Pedernera led
River Plate to three national
titles during the 1940s.

* The Primera Division is the name of the top pro league in Argentina.
** The Copa Libertadores (Liberators Cup) and Copa Sudamericana
   (South American Cup) are the two top club tournaments in South America.

Kit
The official league equipment of soccer players, including a club's uniform.

National Team
A squad made up of a country's best players. National teams compete in tournaments like the World Cup, which is held every four years.

Youth Program
A soccer training school run by a club for its promising young players.

About the Author

Mark Stewart has been writing about world soccer since the 1990s, including *Soccer: A History of the World's Most Popular Game.* In 2005, he co-authored Major League Soccer's 10-year anniversary book.

Photos are on **BOLD** numbered pages.

About C.A. River Plate

Learn more at these websites:
www.cariverplate.com.ar/en
www.fifa.com
www.teamspiritextras.com